Permeable Divide

ALSO BY ELLEN RACHLIN

Waiting for Here (Finishing Line Press, 2004)
Until Crazy Catches Me (Antrim House, 2008)
Captive to Residue (Flarestack Publishing, 2009)

PERMEABLE DIVIDE

Poems by

Ellen Rachlin

Antrim House
Simsbury, Connecticut

Copyright © 2017 by Ellen Rachlin

Except for short selections reprinted for purposes of
book review, all reproduction rights are reserved.
Requests for permission to replicate should
be addressed to the publisher.

Library of Congress Control Number: 2017940864

ISBN: 978-1-943826-27-8

First Edition, 2017

Book design by Rennie McQuilkin

Front cover painting by Mark Lijftogt,
"Seed Bottle with Ranunculus and Apples"

Author photograph by William Louis-Dreyfus

Antrim House
860.217.0023
AntrimHouse@comcast.net
www.AntrimHouseBooks.com
21 Goodrich Road, Simsbury, CT 06070

For Lauren Rachlin and Nancy Posluns

Acknowledgments

Grateful acknowledgment to the editors of the following publications in which certain poems in this volume first appeared, some in earlier versions:

Art Times: "Changes"
Court Green: "Confident"
Granta and *The Los Angeles Review:* "Supernovae"
The Iconoclast: "The Card Reading"
Literary Imagination: "Measure"
Small Brushes: "Naked at the Fast and French" and "Preserve" (as "Reserve")
Literary Matters: "Business Page," "How to Avoid a Scam" and "Inside"
Obsessed With Pipework: "How to Master the Tango and Make Money"
South Carolina Review: "Orientation" and "Silverback Gorillas"
Westchester Review: "Hope"

The following poems appeared in a chapbook, *Captive to Residue* (Flarestack 2009): "A Universal Turn," "Confident," "Changes," "Family," "Debate" (as "Holding Hands"), "How to Master the Tango and Make Money," "Motherhood," "Naked at the Fast and French," "Preserve," "Reflect," "Soloing," "The Card Reading," "The Promise" and "The Group."

My gratitude to William Louis-Dreyfus and Robert Clawson for their uncompromising standards which provided constant challenge. Thankful acknowledgment also to Elise Paschen, who helped me with the final manuscript, and to C.W.'s writing group for generous input on several of the poems in this collection.

Table of Contents

I. THE CHANGE THAT HARBORS LOSS

Possessions / 4
Supernovae / 5
Away / 6
Card Reading / 7
Silverback Gorillas / 8
Debate / 9
Legacy / 10
Limits / 11
Preserve / 12
The Car Argument / 13
Fight / 14
The Trouble with Advice / 15

II. IT'S ONLY NATURAL

Business Page / 18
How to Master the Tango and Make Money / 20
Orientation / 21
Reflect / 22
Myself / 23
Envy / 24
How to Avoid a Scam / 25
Revolution / 26
Naked at the *Fast and French* / 27
Art Turned into Action / 28
Confident / 29
Measure / 30

III. SEEK NO DEADLINE FOR HOPE

Motherhood / 32
Hope / 33
Families / 34
Changes / 35
Intuition / 36
Emergency Kit / 37
The Group / 38
Inside / 40
Freedom / 41
Soloing / 42
The Promise / 44
Multiverse / 45
Looking In and Out / 46
Permeable Divide / 47

About the Author / 49
About the Book / 50

In the absence of observers, our universe is dead.

– Andrei Linde

Permeable Divide

I. THE CHANGE THAT HARBORS LOSS

Possessions

On the plaza, between four building markers,
a man in bright uniform wields
the tools of his trade: broom and bag.
He leans in to gather tissues marked with tears,
containers unburdened of their freight,
loved but fallen stroller toys,
tickets slipped from shallow pockets,
and reams strewn from overflowing trash cans.
On his best days, the plaza gleams,
wiped clean of all origins of hindsight,
carried in the mind's eye but summoned
to barges and carried out to sea.

Supernovae

Theory cannot be tangible fact
like driving on I-95 to get to a lecture
on supernovae with pictures
of white dwarfs sucking mass,
of others fusing hydrogen to their iron cores
before imploding to black.
I'm delayed behind an accident,
one car with a fender blown off,
hanging on the median, driver pacing
the thin turf of tar shoulder,
on a cell phone, mouth gaping
and closing rapidly, hands stitching,
the story part factual, part theoretical.

Away

My house is a maze.
(Look if you wish
as little interrupts me.)
I know the surface
of every wall, each curve,
corner and perch
from which I contemplate Antalya.
The windows are grand
and capture sky to dirt
(though they wear a film of indifference.)
I'm seldom up to breaking out.

The Card Reading

The wintry Norwegian summer drapes snow
across cloudberries. The rolling of our ship
wakes motion sickness in my heart.
Bad weather is useless as sorrow.

The sky is milky all the way to Bodo.
A gypsy deals a paper compass of tarot cards.
The squares are pieces of you
. . . whether on this sea or elsewhere.
Thousands of nesting seabirds circle
like a jumble of papers and dust.
The natural world is never enough.

Silverback Gorillas

It makes perfect sense to walk among them.
They are in our world and we in theirs.
In the distance, soft, round, barely visible,
their movement in the brush is palpable.
As practiced, I move forward—
go clammy, can't hold the gun.

Debate

There is nothing to change
if you fit in,
but that's the catch.
To go from shore to mountaintop
you must adjust.
The mind won't let go.
It puts the absent love's hand
in yours and you grip air.
There is no change
that doesn't harbor loss.
Earth has scarcely changed
though storms cut up the sea.
Yesterday's flat edge is dangerous today—
waiting there, I might be lost at sea.

Legacy

I use a mirror so others
won't see what they might
without my care to shape dress and hair.
I check with chin up, eyes down
and reverse, then with backward glance
I pause to conjure words
should they speak of me.

Limits

Some fears take long to uncover.
The amount of disaster to avoid
climbs to numbers vast as failure.

Mozambique I mulled over,
then scratched off the list I toyed.
Some fears take long to uncover.

Arthritis, stroke *(and always cancer)*
chance that I drop into the void—
climbs to numbers vast as failure.

I fence in what I gather.
Damn hours lost being paranoid!
(Some fears take long to uncover.)

Losing pride doesn't get easier
as a new terror is employed
and joins the numbers vast as failure.

The flawed effort from last year
is another gamble once enjoyed.
Some fears take long to uncover
then yield a mountain vast as failure.

Preserve

Good friends and I drive past Tully Lake.
I desert them
for lakes in other places.
This one with moss,
this one with flowerless lilies,
this one, stone steps,
this, the whir of an engine slowing,
a just tied-up boat bobbing,
the tang of gasoline,
the summer of no year—
my dark and smooth memorial.

The Car Argument

Again the flint for the argument:
her eyes and hands no longer nimble,
unreliable like a train near a faulty switch.
Her voice arcing over her trembling hand
with only her intent firm
as the metal of the keys in her fist.
She is the last of them so I too hold firm.

Fight

I scream.
I can't afford
persuasion's sluggishness
or believe
in empathy.
But within
my pandemonium,
I still wish
you'd understand.

The Trouble with Advice

You and I choose illuminations when we travel:
churches where sunlight rubs
putty-colored glass into masterpieces,
bridges where daylight skids off silt-laden waters,
and narrow streets the day still slithers through.

With our love of clarity
we lavish advice on one another.
But how long do we have until we uncover
the risk of losing one another
by not doing as each instructed?

II. IT'S ONLY NATURAL

Business Page

About currency values
there are many theories including
purchasing power of parity,
trade balance and capital flows,
real interest rates, growth rates
or prospective growth rates,
which were invented to explain
how to think about
how money flows
and why we pay
what we pay for scarcity.

None of these explain why,
if great poems are scarce,
the price to read one
is less than a tomato.
Perhaps one says it's art
and art is meant to be shared
not something hoarded
like money that we think of
as tomorrow's food
or a house in the country
or medicine. To read a poem

never reaches the price
of an opera ticket or a great painting
not even if cherished or rare.
And the price is no different
for a bad poem than
for a great one, unlike meals,
although the cost may be higher.

How to Master the Tango and Make Money

Hyperbolic geometry is understood best
in two dimensions.

Construct a non-Euclidean plane
with lines for endeavors
and only one point for goals.

Goals prevent doubt,
so define for each pursuit.

Don't identify motives.
Triangles with the same angles
don't hold the same area.

In this geometry,
all straight lines converge.

Orientation

The naturalness of natural numbers
comes from their order.
The sense of being > or <
but not = is (no wonder)
natural to us. We need to know
who's ahead, what's behind.

Reflect

I bear the view in a reflecting glass.
Once I tried a grown up hat,
floppy, so I could hardly see.
Now, when I pause and pose to verify,
the parent of the girl is me.

Myself

When I look
right away I adjust my hair
which doesn't stay still,
acts like wisps of smoke.
My neck too stiff and still
I force side to side.
My eyes, light as sea glass,
are rimmed in red.
(I reach for drops.)
My nose is passable, though
faint wrinkles surround it,
encircling my lips.
My covered arms will do
though not too fashionable.
I cannot see myself
for all these interruptions.

Envy

Envy comes between us,
bright enough to shrink the flaw,
either not seen
or like an echo
(not quite as loud).

What I admire, done
by skill or luck, seems
more effortless than
my rigid smile.

I dream of starfruit and alocasia
when races can't be won.

How to Avoid a Scam

Embrace uncertainty—
certainties get scammed.
Even among the good guarantees
scams lurk.
Also avoid promises—you could lose
your life savings
and always your heart.

Revolution

Unaware,
we tangle with ideas
that already have
white hair.

Naked at the *Fast and French*

The real name's *Maliclet*'s.
We call it *Fast and French*.
It's where a customer can order
very French:
fromage du jour,
or not: fondue.
I thought fondue was Swiss
not French except they serve
it up with wine.
I get there *nu*é at ten a.m.
for carrot cake.

Art Turned into Action

In the hall of still life paintings,
visitors trace the light
that creates quince, oyster,
pumpkin, trout, plate, vase
and mottled tabletop
before visiting the café
to tear the flesh of an orange.

Confident

What's more I learned to cook—
now I carry spices on my tongue
and no pens for directions.
How confidently I go.

After plans for company,
days in making, I'm burned
from tossing pyramids
of greens and salt in a hot wok.
My frenzied hands flutter onions and pork
to place on dumpling dough.

At dinner though, I can count on praise.
Who knows my potential?
Any dish is my best.

Measure

The things we try to map:
one town taken in
from a railcar seat,
a sea absorbed
from a deck-side perch,
a distant mountain range
measured between fingertips,
the universe (let's name it time)
seeping through polished glass,
the mystery in myth,
moral boundaries formed in fables,
and for infinity, ∞.

III. SEEK NO DEADLINE FOR HOPE

Motherhood

The science of human birth
seems no different from
the origins of Earth.
Each must wait their turn.
One month is not enough
for hope to acquiesce to loss.
Failure had the stronger case.
Regret became the final stop.
Shortly after I gave in, I celebrated life.

Hope

is larger than now, certainly
than angels, the heft of talismans,
any pain or truth,
and more miraculous than miracles,
the natural world that crawls
across a leaf, generosity, or illusion.

Seek no deadline for hope,
the counterpoint to time;
when placed side by side,
time becomes hope's predator.

Families

Those slack wire acts that balance
by focusing near, love the sloped wire.
First, there are the shakes of contorting bodies,
then the hold while they juggle troubled kin
in each outstretched hand.

The high wire acts with their rigid backs
place the center of their mass
above their distant, chaotic homes
by holding heavy poles
with weights on both ends.

Each act loves how they balance.
Only guilt can make them wobble.
They build a better tribe,
a better routine, or a better home
by trying not to fall.

Changes

Sights like these give me comfort:
my mother's kitchen basket, now in mine;
dance notation from a Robbins' piece;
a teaspoon grained with sugar.

I suffer little things like these
the way the broken-hearted do
love songs:
a crash from a toppled vase,
a meteor shower that clouds erase.

Intuition

Where intuition rules,
even if I want to explain,
there are few facts to share
just hidden connections
to and from the kingdom of senses
as I ease toward happiness.
Yet, I'd gladly sacrifice
this wisdom to take a few more risks—
to have memory and sorrow
completely lost together.

Emergency Kit

Today I need:
food, a place indoors,
some outdoor air,
a book, clean clothes,
and a paycheck
to cover all that.
But I have:
savings, unworn suits,
unread books,
and a contact list
with names I haven't
called in years—
just in case.

The Group

I.

With a datebook in her purse,
so she won't feel alone,
Alice travels.
She phones us from
freeways and airplanes.

Alice has been sailing.
She navigates, compares
her yacht to others.
She's surprised, off course.

II.

Myra confides her affairs
to be confided in
so she can break her word.

III.

Habits draw Lucille.
Her fingers like spiders grope
for scotch and cigarettes.

If we listen when she speaks,
Vivian turns her back
halfway through her sentence.

Mary rigs agreements,
unfastening that clip
where all of us have hung.

Mary always forgives Vivian,
who carries Lucille's number
to interpret her dreams.

Inside

It takes time to notice wallflowers
and longer still to know us.
One needs a sense of purpose
not at first needed to recognize what's missed,

or to see inside all our movement and chatter
the thought that keeps us so well hidden.

Freedom

For a beginning, the horizon is too small,
too low and long, impenetrable.
Deflation whirls,
grazing the narrows' gray palette.
No reference.
Too much frictionless speed
on vectors scarcely known,
but how little can be said
about how freedom chooses.

Habit is a silencer.
The ideal, iced over.
Once my palms bore the wheel,
I drove through endless days
narrower than the past.
To go forward, one must hold on.

Soloing

The morning sky spills fuchsia.
Waves fold over the edge of my craft.
I come about, then jibe a cautious triangle.
The wind picks up, chills the damp of my legs.
A heron circles once, then abandons the watch.
The distant piers frame a labyrinth.

I tack through this liquid labyrinth,
grasp the main sheet until my grip turns fuchsia.
Rescue me? It's only noon on my watch.
The current pulls west and turns my craft.
The trembling barely eases in my legs
as I glide downwind along one side of a triangle.

I raise the spinnaker to a bloated triangle
and try to command the whole labyrinth
no matter how winds alter a trip's legs,
rendering useless routes mapped in fuchsia.
Soloing is my way to learn this craft,
I think more clearly without a critic's watch.

I have done my time under a coach's watch,
studying books on the shapes of the triangle,
listening to sailors praise their craft
after championships in the labyrinth,
and bearing orders from faces in angry fuchsia.
Soloing leads to mastery of any journey's legs.

Sailors, as crews, face difficult legs,
depend on one another to keep the watch,
they cover the deck like wind-stirred fuchsia,
weaving under the sail's triangle.
The crew sails their leader's labyrinth.
Theory asserts this improves their craft.

Partners make me second-guess my craft.
I wait for their calls to change legs
as they lead me through the labyrinth.
Partners may ease the harshness of a watch.
I've been out too far in the triangle,
when the sky turns a stormy fuchsia.

When I master the craft, I'll thread the winds' labyrinth
with a calm watch from day until evening's fuchsia,
the bow ceaselessly triangulating its watery legs.

The Promise

What you might claim
was casual talk, I hold
whole and unrevised.
Now it taunts, with
lack of gesture in between.
I bid your promise up,
more perfect, precious—
the measure of my fragility.

Multiverse

Two lights like stars float below the windowsill.
The possum's eyes catch a certain light
and me half-awake, pushing myself to bed.

I will only find by chance
what moves across my yard at night,
and if the multiverse exists,
it's seeing, not belief, that tells me so.

Looking In and Out

Those who peer into cosmic microwaves
long enough to see primeval atoms
or sort through neural networks
to understand why early memory gets lost
differ from those who
on some evenings join the crowd
in the night sky and find the day ahead
eventful enough.

Permeable Divide

We are together in a galaxy called Loss.
Because I know nothing other than time and place
and where to go to speak with you,
I invented one for you.
No light, no atmosphere needed
to be who you once were.

Since there's no fooling grief,
and remembering is also what I do,
forcing thought to etch you into sight,
there is no time, no nothing—
just spaces collapsed into immortality.

ABOUT THE AUTHOR

Ellen Rachlin is the author of *Until Crazy Catches Me* and two chapbooks, *Waiting for Here* and *Captive to Residue*. Her poems have appeared in various journals and anthologies including *American Poetry Review*, *Granta*, *Literary Imagination*, *Confrontation*, *The Los Angeles Review* and *Court Green*. She received her M.F.A. from Antioch. She serves as Treasurer of The Poetry Society of America and works in finance.

This book is set in Garamond Premier Pro, which had its genesis in 1988 when type-designer Robert Slimbach visited the Plantin-Moretus Museum in Antwerp, Belgium, to study its collection of Claude Garamond's metal punches and typefaces. During the mid-fifteen hundreds, Garamond—a Parisian punch-cutter—produced a refined array of book types that combined an unprecedented degree of balance and elegance, for centuries standing as the pinnacle of beauty and practicality in type-founding. Slimbach has created an entirely new interpretation based on Garamond's designs and on compatible italics cut by Robert Granjon, Garamond's contemporary.

To order additional copies of this book
or other Antrim House titles, contact the publisher at

Antrim House
21 Goodrich Rd., Simsbury, CT 06070
860.217.0023, AntrimHouse@comcast.net
or the house website (www.AntrimHouseBooks.com).

•

On the house website
in addition to information on books,
you will find sample poems, upcoming events,
and a "seminar room" featuring supplemental biography,
notes, images, poems, reviews, and
writing suggestions.